Red Panda

Series "Fun Facts on Zoo Animals for Kids"

Written by Michelle Hawkins

Red Panda

Series "Fun Facts on Zoo Animals for Kids"

By: Michelle Hawkins

Version 1.1 ~March 2021

Published by Michelle Hawkins at KDP

Red Panda's other names are fire car, firefox, lesser Panda, red cat-bear, and red bearcat.

Red Pandas can eat up to 20,000 bamboo leaves daily.

There are less than 10,000 Red Pandas left in the world.

Red Pandas have been around since the thirteenth century

Red Pandas are the only living member left of the Ailuridae family.

Red Pandas are not related to Pandas but rather to skunks and raccoons.

When baby Red Pandas are born, they are grey with thick fur.

Red Pandas are known to be very shy.

During the heat of the day, Red Pandas will relax and sleep; most active in the morning and at night.

Red Pandas spend 90% of their time in trees.

A baby Red Panda weighs 3.5 ounces at birth.

The Firefox web browser used a Red Panda as their logo.

When born, Red Pandas are both blind and deaf.

The average life span of a Red Panda is about eight years.

The tear tracks on a Red Pandas eyes help keep the sun out.

Red Pandas are reddish-brown in color.

To help hold onto bamboo sticks, Red Pandas have two thumbs.

The female Red Panda takes care of the young.

Red Pandas enjoy playing around.

The tail on a Red Panda is used to help keep them warm.

The ankle on Red Pandas can turn 180° to help with movement.

Red Pandas are known to be solitary animals.

The tail on a Red Panda is used for balance.

Baby Red Pandas open their eyes after about three weeks.

The nose on a Red Panda is black.

Red Pandas have been known to have escaped from several zoos.

Red Pandas recognize others by their smell.

Red Pandas are found in Bhutan, China, Himalayas, India, Myanmar, and Nepal.

The average weight for Red Pandas is between six to thirteen pounds.

A baby Red Panda is called a cub.

The claws on Red Pandas help to strip bamboo leaves.

The majority of a Red Pandas diet is bamboo leaves.

The claws on a Red Panda are used for climbing and protection.

The average litter size for Red Pandas is between one to four babies.

Red Pandas have retractable claws, like a cat.

Red Pandas communicate with others through their voice and body movement.

The tail on a Red Panda is between eleven to twenty-three inches long.

The white on the face of a baby Red Panda lights up at night.

Red Pandas are considered endangered.

Red Pandas are very quiet animals.

Red Pandas do not like water and are not good swimmers.

Baby Red Pandas stay with their mom until the new babies arrive.

97% of a Red Pandas diet consists of bamboo.

Red Pandas are considred mammels.

Red Pandas spend up to thirteen hours each day eating and looking for food.

The outside temperature where Red Pandas thrive at is between 63° and 77° F.

The length of a Red Pandas is between twenty to twenty-five inches long.

Red Pandas were given their name before the actual Panda was named.

Red Pandas talk to others by squeaking and whistling.

Red Pandas are pregnant for three months.

Since Red Pandas live in trees, they are considered arboreal.

sl

The fur covering Red Pandas feet is for insulation and grip.

Red Pandas are easy to blend in due to the trees with moss.

The nest that is used for baby Red Pandas is made up of grass and twigs.

The tail on a Red Panda is long and shaggy.

Red Pandas will go down a tree headfirst.

Red Pandas are one of the only mammals that enjoy drinking aspartame, an artificial sweetener.

Red Pandas have black eyes.

Fire fox means Red Panda.

Red Pandas lick themselves like cats to keep clean.

The ears on a Red Panda are always at attention and upright.

Red Pandas are very territorial.

Red Pandas are bigger than a cat.

When cold, Red Pandas become as slow as sloths.

Baby Red Pandas do not come out of their nest till they are three months old.

Red Pandas are known to be very mischievous.

To drink water, Red Pandas will dip their paws into it.

Red Pandas have a round head.

During the day, you can find a Red Panda in a tree sleeping away.

The legs in the front of a Red Panda are shorter than their back legs.

In most zoos, you will find a Red Panda.

Find me on Amazon at:

https://amzn.to/3oqoXoG

and on Facebook at:

https://bit.ly/3ovFJ5V

Other Books by Michelle Hawkins

Series

Fun Facts on Birds for Kids.

Fun Fact on Fruits and Vegetables

Fun Facts on Small Animals

Fun Facts on Dogs for Kids.

Fun Facts on Dates for Kids.

Fun Facts on Zoo Animals for Kids.

Made in United States
Troutdale, OR
12/02/2023

15244505R00021